MW00478484

WHATEVER TIME WE LIVE

Also by the Author:

Joseph's Son
Braver Than That
Songs for Wanderers

WHATEVER TIME WE LIVE

SHEILA MOON

THE GOLDEN QUILL PRESS
Publishers
Francestown   New Hampshire

Library of Congress Catalog Card Number 82-82297

ISBN 0-8233-0347-0

Printed in the United States of America

To the Mother of Earth,
Rocks, Death, Seed, Birth.

CONTENTS

I. Some Winding Way

II. Alone. Apart.

III. Bearing Witness

IV. Single Truth

I.   SOME WINDING WAY

CHOICE

If we are bidden to let go
of all we have held
(by acts and accidents and falls
from grace), if dreams
have hidden themselves by night
and a felled tree
glows with strange lights,
if we see our faces
in fire, in snow, and
in cold springs of time and pain —
what we have then is choice
between vain desires
to be ringed by love,
and voiceless willingness to live
higher than wish.
Our years, haggard, proud,
give not rest nor resolution
but crowd into us, filling us,
while each hour lags behind
and our best is tears.

O lovely dove, murmuring
minor songs into May sky,
unfold my hands, find me
a long day, unhurt and standing
clean, vivid, lined
with golden petals and trees
of silver! Bird, I would hold
only one flower (a tiny weed
in rose) only one hour
and then my hand let go.

GROUNDSEL CHILDLEAF

Anywhere is a groundsel childleaf sleeping
if you watch where your feet go, letting your eyes
navigate your heart. Sable pools keep
strange roots underground, tended by those wise
enough to stay small, gnarled, and hidden.
Such ones grow slant, ploughing wild fields
where nothing is but yellow groundsel bidden
by dwarf gods to be childleaf, and to yield
its innocence only to those who, sleeping, dream
they wander underearth seeking a silver child
in darkness. To find such in moon's beam,
curled in its polished leaf, is a joy wild
as a winter wind and soft as a caress.
Anywhere is a groundsel childleaf asleep
until you can seek it out, until you can bless
its existence and yet its silvered silences keep.

REDEMPTION

"With Time, Your gift",
I wander a fool's field of stars,
lifting each one for light
to see by. But breathing darkness
is not to be requited. It abides.
There is rime on weeds.
Arcturus is high, cold. My mode,
endless as any other, older
than earth, is tended by death
which leads evermore to birth.

"Let me redeem the time" of
becoming, of freedom and love,
of all prime valiant battles, of sun
and moon in their forever dance.
Whoever calls, let me go willing,
soon, taking my lance and lute,
my falcon on my gloved hand.

    And
"lest my day of grace be lost"
and I be tossed on a shore
of stones, a place of shattering,
let me be lonely, be filled
with more portents and matters
of wonder than I have known
before. Let me be love,
be wanderer, be pulchinella,
let me be under obedience
to Time, Your gift, until
my day of grace is done.

EMPTY POCKETS

To drink a life to its full measure
(savoring ebony at each cups end)
means a willingness not to be sure
of any shining height of time. To bend
hours or years for my desire's sake
is impossible. I'm learning to give
whatever comes its option to take
capacity, and thus what space I live
is every space not held by my desire.
It feels as a hawk must, against sun —
high and alone and nimbused in fire —
crying whatever freedom has been won.
"Empty your pockets," said my dream.
Let go of earth, of gravity, of place,
and rise with feathered bones to gleam
for a single moment on earth's face.

ON A PORTUGUESE BEACH

A smiling smooth skull
   I will also be —
later than you, bird,
   but will be.
And whatever else?
Thought, dream,
   rain in gray air,
      sounds, as bird song
or the sea?
Whatever else?

Skull with a name,
whose name have you?

"Yours", it smiles.
"Yours,
God's trouble!"

I cover your mouth,
skull.
      Stop crying!
       Stop!

It will not stop,
neither for me, bird,
nor for you.
It echoes tides and tumults.
It keeps on crying
     "You!
       Your name!
       Whatever else but
         You! You!"

SHARED BALLADE

I cannot share your tumulted rough seas,
or know those gulfs which terrify your days.
I cannot feel what brings you to your knees.
But I've my inward hours of fear and praise
(lonely often, anguished, yet ever amazed
at life's tormented joy). These help me guess
what courage is required from you to blaze
your road towards where the Word can bless.

Each life is solitude. Also some things stay —
we've each our inward hours of fear and praise,
our knowing that love withstands every duress
and that each road leads to where Love can bless.

THE YEAR THE ANTS BROUGHT THE BONES

It was a tenth year, strange, thunder
in June rumbling over summer.
We had been many months away.
Birds were building in usual ways
hearing sun rise and set, asleep
in moonlight. Ants did not keep
the faith, though. Night after night
they harried your grave. No sight
was possible into their tunnels.
Mindless, silent, they funneled
seeds down and weed husks slowly
up to cover stones, to lay snow
circling their castle door.
On your death day, long before
light, they came with bone,
bits of a dark sea's foam.
I knelt in hot sun, bright,
to gather mined ivory, white
as festivals. Your birthday.
The ants have gone away.

ROUNDABOUT

Waking to stillest trees ghosted
against pewter sky, I'm caught between night
and again. The pygmy owl calls
its last belled serenade. Bright-
ly a lantern, Venus stands alone.
Orion has vanished. Death
prefaces often in this spectral hour
between now and next, where breath
is slow, known is lost, where body
resents its work and spirit reaches
towards happier places of nothing,
where "done" is not, "undone" beached
as a wrecked boat. But waking is
honest, resist or take. And, when sun
again discovers this rotating earth,
dying dies reluctant and living runs
on until another roundabout is done.

STONE

Somewhere inside me is
a round small stone of
mica and diorite.
It is bright and dark.
For over twenty five
thousand long days
it has turned, soundless,
stark — turned with ice,
with tears, with fire,
with storm and loneliness,
with joys warmed by love,
and perhaps, above all,
with staying persistent
(though wrong as often as right)
for some later day and night.

BURRS

The dog sheds burrs on my floor.
I gather them up. There is
a moral here: You can go out a door
through which you didn't enter.
From a burr's view, this twist
could mean a bright center
of next year's weeds,
             or death.
My dog cares only that burrs go.
For me, they're irritants. My breath
gets short at all disordered things!
This should not be. I know
it's peril!   Whenever you cling
to a just order its twin revives
and chaos is throned. These burrs,
like my bunglings, if kept alive,
could blossom in some other May
to star a field. It might occur,
who knows. Dog, let us pray.

LEARNING

When lifesize was less
than walking alone to school
my trust was not thin.
Mother meant thereness
and father two smiling arms
to wrinkle me in.

Matters changed — they do,
I learned — like increase
of me, debts, *angst*:
like ugly was mostly true
and everyone worked where
they could and no thanks.

I am now late into time.
Peace and her sister of dark
roam my days of rain
and fire, and falcons climb
skies. I have sculptured love
by learning to chisel pain.

SOME WINDING WAY

I know only that
someone awaited me
in a vast City.
Webs of rails,
canals, highroads,
went towards Always.
Whatever of pity
lay about I
had not access to it.
Alone on routes I
never knew, or
had forgotten,
with muddled mind
and mirror-clear heart
(in Bottom's fashion)
I'd a view of
some winding way of
loneliness. But how,
what, when — then
or now — who or where —
my dream was — but
did not say.

EYES

In pewter dawn owls
send final songs
bouncing through shadows.
Then silence.
Cocks are not alight,
nor dogs, nor daybirds.
I am that singular one,
solitary, voiceless,
a primal thing waiting
for sun to return
my world to shapes known,
to identifiable sounds,
to color.

Predawn monochrome is a
pagan mystery.
My eyes, surprised
by it, want to be cat's eyes.
Such magic is brief, unsure,
kin to faces of small children
or to young animals with
virginal eyes unlidded
in contemplation of scenes
past any vision of mine.
Perhaps death opens
one singular hour for us
to step into this lovely
silverblack stillness,
to see owls singing gold,
to feel veins of trees lift
life from ground to crown,

and to share earth's trembling
before that restive passion
of what is to be.

NIGHT WANDERER

From buried silences of deep sleep
dreaming dawn power mostly comes
in slivers of sunfire, steep
as firtips against silver air.
Waking arises in me as a death.
I turn my eyes inside. A bird runs
on my roof — and what does it do there,
I wonder, refusing morning's gold.
It sings without taking a breath,
an orange-silver tune of light.
Laughing, I bring myself to be bold
enough to risk another span of hours
— to sing, to work, to honor flowers,
to love, again to wander into night.

SUNRISE POOL

I see myself adrift
in a sunrise pool,
charcoal shadow laid
on shimmer, a fool
holding circles, lifting
aureoles of dark shade
and first light as if I
made them. Absurd,
this image. A nought
of God is neither sky
nor sun, nor sound heard
from elsewhere. Brought
to a sunrise pool awry,
voiceless, I am dark
against light, I am old,
I am child, I am lark
skyborn, foolishly bold,
I am funeral barque
for Osiris, am death
shimmering in turquoise
inlaid with bright bone.
I see myself as breath
lost in sunrise, noiseless
as spiders, shining, alone.

ALONE

What does 'alone' tell?
It tells me. It says
'be born'. And 'die'. A singular well,
it is empty for endless days.
Then, in capricious spring
of dream, it is brim-filled
with mythic sounds and rings
of magic. It leads uphill
where wind blows and flowers unfold,
where rabbits are joying in green,
where I must find gold.
'Alone' tells of things unseen.
It is austere as a resting cat,
claws sheathed but primed.
It says die and be born. That
is how we outguess Time.

COUNTERPOINT

A full draft of darkness
approaches me, with that deep
contrapuntal canon singing
from a lonely ocean's sleep.
My world's withdrawal brings
awareness of a flood tide,
of an encroaching time —
and rocks — weathered, stark
menhirs on far moors to hide
fairy rings and those long dead.
My life runs as an infant wind
through marsh reeds, and red
is each dawn. I am afraid.
Also I know my voice has been
singing in silence has made
love into waiting, tears into seed.
It is a loneliness of coming,
a way not chosen yet one to heed
for life's sake. My heart runs
with God, with patterns of desire
not known before. To go into shade
is to listen for that silent Fire
by Whom this universe was made.

HEART CAN BECOME

What an incredible breaking
is a heart as it falls
into black seas, making
no sound, never calling
to an abyssal night
but letting old forms
become a fiery flight
of particles — free, warm,
open to being anywhere
and loved by what needs
to love. Heart can ride air,
water, and earth. Freed
from belonging and desire,
heart can become God's fire.

II.   ALONE.   APART.

ALONE. APART.

Whenever you see a stream
too hidden for sharing —
burn to solitude and dream
until, sudden, it leaps into air —
a stream held between stones
and freefalling through mist
into a grey-green pool alone —
then follow each upward twist
to those lonely, brooding heights
above timberline. Alone. Apart.
When you come, watch sun's light.
See how it enters your heart.
      Here will be hawk, will be dove.
      Here will be cleansing of love.

THE WALKERS

i

Apollo, walker of dawn-light hills,
walker of mighty stones,
of dolphin-singing waves,
help us to set our feet —
as privy as you did —
on whatever ring of earth we have.
Help us to walk strong,
singing gold songs for birth.

ii

To walk through tended fields
is to learn grain and grape
                    as long journeys.
Their infant standing is green.
Riding seasons to gold, to purple,
their song of pride is elegy.
                    They die.
Beaten. Crushed. Trampled. Threshed.
Where autumn wind walks, they are not.
Empty are sunlit earth and vine,
a hush fills furrows.
They gave us leave to take them
                    and make miracles
of bread and wine,
rebirths at the end of journeys,
                    blessed from pain to praise.
We raise them and begin to walk again.

iii

Dionysos, walker and wanderer
among passionate vines, come singing,
                come singing!
Come ringed with moonburnt fire,
sound ankle bells on naked feet
that we may follow a boy god
                bringing purple stars.

iv

A river knows its sources, its sea.
It stumbles from snowbank or spring
downhill, earth's urchin
trying out crevice to crack to cleft.
Its childhood left, it hurries on
ringing pebbles as streams,
impetuous often, sometimes filled
                with dreams.
A river's a walker,
as it grows old. Torrent, flood,
rapids and waterfalls are known.
It breathes sea winds and moves
meandering to meet them. It sees
its life entire, and peaceful flows
                toward its final fire.

v

High walks the hawk in hot sky.
Bird of gods, sword-bladed bird
roaming lonely space, how are we
repeated in your eyes?

Our faces
looking down, feet beneath our heads,
flat beetles we must seem to you
who walk a red sunrise.

EVENING GROSBEAKS

These birds come gaily to our April tree,
sending soft calls from branch to bough,
dropping, climbing, and then falling free.

Our great oak in its splendor lets them be.
Whatever they wish to do it will allow
as they come gaily to our April tree.

They rustle, they stretch, trying to see
what they have overlooked. They preen and bow,
dropping, climbing, and then falling free.

Handsome they are, with a rich modesty
sounding their gentle calls. All world is now,
as birds come gaily to our April tree.

With their blunt bounce there is beauty
around them — I can't describe just how —
in dropping, climbing, and then falling free.

Holding their flock together faithfully
they wander spring pink woods and out
as they come gaily to our April tree.

They move in quiet and graceful glee
as if they know what this life is about.
Dropping, climbing, and then falling free
these birds come gaily to our April tree.

A SEASHORE IS WAITING

Take cradle endlessly rocking, set it down
on some river of silver and green light.
A seashore is waiting, lonely, blown.

Plovers measure its tidal inlets around,
marking that pool where tenebral nights
take cradle endlessly rocking, set it down.

Infancy died. Ghosted in casket brown
it flees through granite canyons to where, white,
a seashore is waiting, lonely, blown.

These final sands slope gently as a gown
to clothe a corpse. All slow twilights
take cradle endlessly rocking, set it down.

Each sanderling and every gull not flown
into darkness calls a full moon, bright.
A seashore is waiting, lonely, blown.

Nightbirds, chant elegies of your own
for the newly dead to still its flight;
take cradle endlessly rocking, set it down.
A seashore is waiting, lonely, blown.

SAW WHET OWLS

Sky is a misted-moon silver
embroidered with pinetree black
when my saw whet owls come home.
Their song is flute's low notes
bubbling through velvet. Only
two handspans around, they turn
their faces upside down to measure
me. (I'd like to see me so!)
Golden-eyed lamps in dawn light,
their soft bright water music
is a muted fanfare calling day.

HERON

A cross salmon mist of light
a great blue heron rows
her curved ship in silent skies
above our venerable oak —
a regal Isis on a sacred lake,
moving rich and softly slow
toward hills of pines breaking
open a silver dawn. No
slightest sounds of moving wings
stir silence above or below
her going. Such birds as sing
before sunup are doing so,
while she in stillness unrolls time.
Last summer's nest, let go,
has fallen. Somewhere another pine
holds young. The heron knows.

NOT YET

"Not yet!" shouts September,
"I'm not that old!"
But we are. We've reasons
for wanting cold.
November routs those shades
that haunt a dying year.
I'm not sure why, unless
this old month says birth
is near. Let's play the fool,
then, singing carols when earth
is yet bronze, orange, ochre,
cool blue — and the ring
of twelve has still a turn to go.

THREE

I found a small green frog,
gleaming as a jewel might,
under my desk. It was dead.
A crippled mouse I tended,
watching through each night
for its faint stirs, its head
as small as a doll's tucked
under its tail. Life ended
in late afternoon. A bird,
small and golden green,
encountered a window glass
and no one ever heard.
We buried them, each one,
(from water, earth, and air).
Having no salamander from sun
or fire we had to do with three.

A MOTH TREE

Day by day it is a pendant
    of old twisted fig wood
hung outside our window to keep
birds from immolation.
    Darkness makes magic of it.
    Indoors a tabled candelabra mimics
wood's shape with creation
of flames on its branch ends.
It is a nightly minor pentecost.
The moths come — silent, huge-eyed,
agitated bodies of longing to quit
their solitude.
    Unreachable fires
pull them, demanding as gods.
They pause, quivering against glass,
their fragile bodies go lower, higher,
branch to branch to branch.
Fervent is their passion
    for light, for light,
        for that tree of light
at their eyes' edges, wings' tips,
    so brightly is it
kept from them. Slowly they weary,
    some die,
and a few velvetgray ghosts
plead until day, then disappear.

SEA OTTERS

A breathing tide lifts shine of weeds
holding to rock matrix distances down.
Cradled thus, these infants of sea,
these round-eyed balls of golden brown,
contemplate mother diving in shadowed blue.
She becomes all ripple and trusted buoy
and sea urchin finder and servant to
their bright eagerness and hungry joy.
Kelp cradle rocks them, that heartbeat
of their birth. Ocean is gentle here,
melting to sky and rocks and sweet
with sun and starlight and no fear.

　　No human ever had such form or face.
　　These must be children of gods of grace.

LETTING LIFE BE

Letting life be, I rest in such shade
as our December oaks provide. Acorns made,
trees rest as their leafed hands grow old
and wrinkled and ready for cold.
Such dying is accepted graciously,
                              letting life be.

Our uncommon acorns are polished jade.
Our prevailing ones begin to fade
into receptive ground. Sunlight is bold
but diminished. A year is almost told.
Its quietude is steady, faithfully
                              letting life be.

47

WINTER

This winter of our year has come
suddener than foreseen — ground
not prepared quite, storm windows
where they were put in early spring,
and some roses will of course be lost.
We should have been more ready.

Winter's been premature before. Ready
means to recall, not to dream and come
startled, innocent, hurt that lost
sunlight won't return, that ground
underfoot is alien, not fitting spring,
that we can't see for ice on windows.

Outlook and insight equally need windows.
Nestlings need shelter, only later are ready
to fly. I fear we fastened to spring,
let bright summer and autumn smoke come
when we were not there. Thus time, ground,
blossoms, fruits, burning leaves are lost.

We cannot turn time around. What is lost
is forever. This present is outside all windows.
What path we walk is on present ground,
and if we are stunned to silence or ready,
it does not matter. All seasons come
turning — summer, autumn, winter, spring.

And it is winter. Nothing makes it spring.
Wasps' nests fall. Long afternoons are lost

to twilight, malefic toadstools come
mounded and poisonous, all windows
are streaked with cold rain, already
our longest night approaches burial ground.

Making lament, we can honor now this ground
of necessary sleep. Despite ourselves, we see spring
as it has been and maybe can be, ready
for unseen seeds. We can perhaps cherish lost
and unremembered things, even storm windows,
for winter is here, the time already come.

> Come! See prefaces of spring —
> ground cracked, not all green lost,
> windows frost polished and ready.

III. BEARING WITNESS

BEARING WITNESS

Invaded, tormented, orphaned,
wandering — what can we do?
We try to fight back
        with love
            a non-lethal weapon.
And wider spaces, gently purpled
ranges of hills   free
somewhere deer, foxes, racoons,
        air pure with sun,
            songs of parenting birds —
all this argues lostness and orphans,
yet doesn't.
        Makes it sharper, poignant,
for love feels so passionately loving
and so passionately impotent
"in a dry year"
with glaciers and deserts advancing.
Sorrow in golden sap rising
        falling,
            rising,
                falling,
tree's fervent desire to be,
that surprise of all existences
            at death.
Sorrow ploughs a soil rich
with humus of thousands of years,
        and fears,   tears,
and our goodnesses rent apart.
So be it.
If "my head were waters, and

mine eyes a fountain of tears",
I could be clean at last,
purged of a lifetime's scum,
could rise, a newborn spring
        laughing.
If she could weep, they said.
she could love, they said.
My Lord Dunsany had a point.

American Indians kept reverence
a bright thread
        as they wove themselves
into their bounteous earth,
blessing it,
        planting feathers on treetips
                when they killed.

Destruction for us is a way of being.
Why must Parsifal's passion
        be so cruelly laid against death?
Or —
        it comes out of dying
with sweetness of small lilies in May —
        is that the way of it?
How we resolve destruction?
Together with trees
        rippling bird songs
                into air as warm, as clear,
as bright as on that primal day?
        And yet
destruction for us is a way of being,
written into our paradox
                forever insoluble,

as love also is insoluble
but, like air, forever needed to breathe.

In any event we are each one
        at the last alone.
Will it seem small, that final space,
or endless and shimmering phosphorescence
of sea under moonlight?
whichever — or other — who will witness that?

Nightly my dog and I
measure,   unhurried,
        (lamp post
                to captive tree
                        to patch of refuse
                                etcetera)
our swatch of the city.
It is small in many dimensions.
Condominiums have guards
        and enough cement each
for a hospital and a graveyard.
Dignified residences from another history
on their hills
        remain elite with one name
or harbor nameless communes.
                Cities,   like lives,
                tend to come apart as
                        age
                            limps
                                    down.
My dog and I walk alone
concentrating on small tasks.

We cannot bear witness to larger ones,
not in this stranger-night
of icy winds from the sea.

A YEAR

This year is not wider in time, but has a bite
of movement slower than joy, faster than cure,
leading towards darkness as deep as any night.

I walked Greece again. Sounion's gloried white
was smudged. Only asphodels stood brief and pure.
This year is not wider in time, but has a bite.

Ancient temples persist, with seas, but human blight
goes faster than they. Death alone is secure,
leading towards darkness as deep as any night.

I worry words, trying to help them come right,
to be voices of need. It does not go. I abjure.
This year is not wider in time, but has a bite.

Planet and I are older. We should have a right
to be told of our fate. Nobody seems sure.
This year is not wider in time, but has a bite
leading towards darkness deeper than any night.

HAPPENINGS

When events begin only to happen
        we,
           then,
are irrelevant
and where history is concerned
        we
like the dinosaurs
are better extinct
because
        we
even as they
are no longer pliable and
cannot choose to be different when
circumstances change
like too many births or an ice age
        and we are crushed
by happenings that have stopped being events
        and when we
have electrified computerized chemicized
earth into surrender
        and expanded ourselves
with nuclear weaponry   alki   TV   speed   success
        grass   and all
other transfers of responsibility
history too will
be a happening in past tense.

DROUGHT

It was a parched season. Trees
and weeds grew juiceless too soon.
Terse rain pocked the earth
briefly twice and departed. Heat
was weighty and solid as rock.
Even a full moon seemed withered.
                    All pain
was italicized   every spring
bereaved   faces made small.
More birds died against glass,
deceived by mirrored-water sky.
                    Dryness
filled us, was food, passed into us
reminding us of our dying.
(I think this is not wrong
                    sometimes
to remember death. Every song
has a first note and an end.)
Mornings were mute   empty stages
with rust trees
                    leaves hung just so.
Slowly heat entered. Aging earth
sees that night's curtain falls
on a repeated scene.
                    All life
grew ashen, while bitter rains
came brief   meaningless.
Greening was lost to pain.

THE TRAIL GOT WIDENED

    because of drought
and because fire might eat
    pine, oak, fir,
    madrona, laurel.
It was rasp, grind, shout
of earth-movers stirring
    roots and rocks
    and branches
into ugliness that my feet
stumbled over, shocked.
The day the trail got widened
it had to be done. Around here
what start fires are people.
    No lightning strikes.
    It's we the people —
driven to excess by our fears,
our sallow lives, our steeples
    of lust and blight
    stabbing our air —
we set the fires, we dress
hills in our burned-out desires.
The day the trail got widened
I walked it wrathful
two-minded about human skill
    and its aftermath
    until grief filled
me with pity and each leaf
was stitching up the path.

ONE CUP OF GREEN

All cities where I've lived
are fringed with ruin —
      houses pockmarked from age
      peevishly peering
      from half-shut eyes;
      incidental patches of earth
      outraged by refuse;
      dry grasses trying to
      birth seeds from broken glass;
      children of many hues
      screaming on streets,
      or, faded and passive,
      wasting their day.

We've nothing in cities to give.

All handles are marked DESTRUCT.

      We have tons of racket,
      tall piles of din,
      and ruckuses enough by darkness
      to drown us in.

Earth, lead us home!
Give us, if we can bear it,
some air, and one cup of green!

NOT YET COLD

The backdrop of earth is still.
I wander in dream among trees.
Movement is only songs of birds —
bright scarlet, rounded gold —
and a small snake riding a hill.
Where do I live? How old
is this world? Has anyone heard?
Spring air flashes with bees.
Can a breathing god fulfil
this season alone, let unfold
richness, and bear the word?
Or teach me meanings for free?
Wind turns winter leaves, a mill
making rich soil. I have heard
earthworms whisper. Grape leaves
against their pewter vines are bold,
shining. I sense I'm very old
from knowing. My life occurred
but once. My love, like gills
of fish, helps me to breathe
as I struggle a world absurd,
lovely, afraid, but not yet cold.

MAY IT BE SO

Can we not somewhen touch spirit
with desiring warm flesh,
bring sunrise to a heart
with flowers as golden fresh
as April overtaking December?
No, we cannot. Hours of time
are not possessed, remember.
They contain things apart
from us — sanderlings sublime
on rolling sand, a giant tree split
from crown to root by storm
standing with comrades yet
in peace, or gnats that swarm
busy spirals above May grass.
Hours of time hold these. We
cannot hold time, cannot pass
twice through this door to see
a year again. As leaves fall
so we, bequeathing to an earth
our acid rain, poisoned air, all
imperishable wastes, each birth
deformed by our superior skills.
Outside my window madronas glow,
quails tiptoe down my leafed hill,
all is in order. May it be so.

DO NOT BE CREDULOUS

Do not be credulous about earth.
It is what we believing in a beginning —
innocently green, and blue-skied,
and waiting only for us to come in
to see marvels. But also there is birth —
raw and blood-stained and crying.
Pain can be forgotten for a time
but is stored, coded in nerve and bone
for recall. We learn this fact
from cold winter with its snow blown
into white desert, its windows rime-
shattered. No possible willed act
of ours can unwind this full turn.
All climates and happenings come,
go, will come again. Pitiless charity,
charitable death, are each names
for our eternal fierce fires which burn
an old year with such brevity.

I've fancied that on some sunrise
near time's edge, existence will glow
in fabulous furnaces of loves and births
so radiant as never to have to know
those imminent ashes and closed eyes.

But do not be credulous about earth.

ARRIVAL AT NOW

Imagining our arrival at Now
is not possible. It is also absurd.
Mists, rain, black blind space,
light points, exploding shining dust,
twisting winds, abysses where motes race —
all this should not be ended with us.
But we are story makers. We heard
that a gleaming rope ascended
to us, and from us. What is how?
And when will it be ended?
How will it? What day will appear
over our ruins to answer why?
And if it knows, can we hear
its forsaken and love lost cry?

NOT QUITE COMPLETE

When alone steps over a threshold to here,
and hounds cease troubling night,
when birds are mute, and cats disappear
from their pleased circles, and a blight
of clouds poisons our usual firmament,
when mind staggers into left and right
turned backward — this is a world bent
into unfamiliar time where ears must see
another light, and eyes reach for scent
of flowers dying under a trembling tree.
It isn't terror that rules. It is what's lost
that has dominion — what could not be
of unborn moments, images that were tossed
away under duress, tantalizing roads
not traveled for fear of larger costs,
and loves left out because of what was owed
elsewhere. Time, images, paths, love —
what must be done for requiem? This load
of unburied corpses, these dead we strive
to put by, their silence is hurting wide
as a thousand children crying above
an apocalypse! We sense we must give pride
away, must 'take our shoes from off our feet'
to stand on this barren ground allied
with commoners of courage who dare meet
their lost, unborn, unclaimed, untaken times,
— tormented, never sure, not quite complete.

MISSA VOX HUMANA

Kyrie

Mercy.   Bright russet-orange leaves
of November silently cover graves.
Fruit falls faithful to time. Rabbit and deer
are profited by this turn of days.
Mercy thus for them. For us, we must
let our seeds fall over an earth,
hungry, desiring something alive to trust,
desiring deaths leading at last to birth.
Mercy. Mercy for that lonely Thing
Who lives within the human heart
beseeching love, a place, to sing
softly sometimes, not to be set apart.

Gloria

Nativities   are   glorys
happening   forever   year   after   year
returning swallows to nests
returning fruit to vines
returning love to spring sunlight,

       or

    to bright winter berries given freely

       or

    to promises kept

       or

    to truths told.
God's glory is to be born,

    over and over to be born from death

as sunrise in fringes of rain,
as spring's first breathing,
as clear skies
   and rivers full, pure, and free
     after anguished droughts of time.
Nativities, happenings, gifts, truths, returnings
   are
   glorys.

Credo

I believe substance and shadow
belong to us as our inheritance
   richly from birth to death
   (and who knows then?)
   and we die
   and live for both
   and perhaps they redeem us.
If we had only half of these —
   either half —
I believe we'd not survive longer
   than a heart beating only one direction.
Sometimes dim, sometimes shining,
we pulsate like fireflies
   unless we are dead.
These things I know from love's lessons.

I believe   that what is, is not,
      because it has not ended,
      that what is not, can be,
      because it has not become.

All events   can become and end
             or end and become
             and which way it goes and why
             depends on how God and human
             relate to each other.
Mostly, I believe these ends and beginnings
             are a human decision.
I believe God is more reliable.

Sanctus

Holiness is a heart's sweep
          across all faces of time passing.
Holiness is what comes
          when nothing seems to be possible.
Holiness is snow on barren trees
          and sunrise with clouds and birds
Holiness is when the God of hosts
          shines in a blade of grass
          or sings in circumpolar winds.

Benedictus

A misted-moon sky filled with owls,
Happy plume of dog's tail,
All acceptances of what is past,
   These are unarmed benedictions.

Possibly any benediction is gratuitous.
Otherwise it would be a purchase.

To be blessed is to be alive,
is to have even a small fragment of time
in which to understand.

To feel a benediction from the Other
is a rich experience —
but sometimes, after giving all It has
to our harried lives, I feel
our benediction is needed by It.

Perhaps every benediction is reciprocal.

DEATH OF THE WORLD

We,
too,
shall die,
passing beneath world's lintel
into rains of God
(lonely a birdless twilight)
and our places know us
no more.

(In noonday
of parched time snow
is driven before blowing sun
over all cracks and crevices and
creatures, all transients
who had thought to be
forever.)

Will then the quick
be killed even before stars fall,
holding in unlikely hands
baskets of spring? And bones
flow before them as
waves in a frozen sea?

We
too
shall die,
held in a giant wonder
that all these brief shut hearts
denying every common grace
could wipe away
the world.

IV. SINGLE TRUTH

SINGLE TRUTH

A lifetime of storm-swept lives
of suns both tight and slack,
days sinking and days rising,
sinking, rising — and nights of moons
bent almost to nothing and back
— these are creation's mayflies
compared to any single truth
which crosses our time's track.
Neither gain nor loss, truth is breath
for gasping light-struck souls
who have lived blind and deaf
until, seared by sudden god-flame,
they come full turn, pay their toll,
follow a road with no name.
Our minds are misfits. Inner sight
tells us an unknown path waits
and can be found, even in night,
and followed, lonely and very late.

THE ASS

(1)

Rounded, sandgray, and softly precise
she was as she waited. Raher the herdsman
stroked her flanks. No wives of rulers
moved as right as she moved. Her eyes
absorbed him. This ass of Balaam —
what could she see that he could not?
Her gaze was all sky and stars singing
and birds running the winds. She could
hear calls from nowhere, pointing her ears
towards emptiness. He knew she could.
"And whatever I am," he thought,
"is hers. That's my distress." Raher
rubbed her satin nose and from his hand
she lipped a fig. He wished he cared less
for her. She belonged to Balaam the mystery,
soothsayer, troubler, who made his own rules
paired with scoundrels and kings. Let him be.

Wandering his variegated herd to remnant fields,
Raher blew a wild spinning birth from pipes,
watching a moon, pale and seductive, in a hot sky.
The ass stood beside him, ears reading him and
something further and larger. How many more
years would pass, he wondered, before he saw
with her seeing, shared her fire?

(2)

Return was a noise of travelers,
summer dust palling the valley.

Soldiers from Moab here?
He folded his herd carefully.
Two nights and a day slaves
and servants rustled events
of masters. Enemies? Friends?
At war? They might. Princes
fetched gold. What is meant
none said. Balaam spoke yes
and no — not usual, said those
who said they knew him best.
After a second night Balaam arose.

(3)

She was so shining, Raher saw,
leading her to the seer.
Saddle of finest wood, raw
soft leather for bridle, no fear
in her anywhere. The lack
was Balaam, Preceding the Moabites.
So sudden she left their track
that Raher gasped. What fright
had taken her? Balaam beat
her flanks. A friend grabbed the boy
Raher. "Don't go! Her feet
are his, not yours! He can destroy!"

She bore him patiently by walls
of a vineyard, then pinned his foot
hard against stone. Raher almost called
but shook his head. "She", he thought,
"sees what we cannot. Let be."
Balaam struck her again and again,

77

but she laid herself quietly
down in dust, showing no pain.

(4)

Balaam came to her raging. Wind rose
screaming from nowhere into a sky
of fire and wings and sun and stars
and a roar of voices. Raher's flock
of sheep and goats watched with serene
wide eyes while worlds blew around them.

In a tombed stillness the ass said,
"Balaam, why beat my body sore?"
"You made me a fool?" His face red,
he threatened to hurt her more.
"I've served, Balaam, all my days."
"You have." His clenched hands dropped.
He knelt beside her, covered his face.
All wind and every murmur stopped.

(5)

It was transfigured then, this time, these shapes,
this common world. No light had ever shone
as lucid as poured in streams from whatever
towered as feathered cumulus above them,
while Balaam wept.

And Raher laughed in love,
seeing little ass and goats and sheep asleep.

JOSEPH

"I will be loneliest.
For me, only a dream
which, oddly, seems true.
But what does God
need an old man to do
for this bursting seed?
Boldly to guard
a first and always guest
for a proper earth?
To serve births in odd places?"

   His face bemused,
his eyes try distant time
and seed wise Sirius.
"Better than sun-fused bleak
skies. There will not be rest,
but hills to be crested
night after night forever.
Filled cups (other than pain)
will not come often. No.
I will be loneliest."

   So why do his eyes,
looking up to raining stars,
grow wider with Yes?

A GOD'S HOME

Alone is being born
in midnight wind and rain
and no shelter, shorn
of stillnesses, blind
from pain of gathering
all sounds and echoes
into a willed emptying of want.
A clown haunts gardens where
once were doves. He knows
love is loneliness and grace
and prayer. His white face
glows in a dark place of trees
where an infant is crying.
Birth — any birth — is stark,
bloody, unseeing. It strives
in night winds, black earth
beneath, cold moon watching,
a fool for midwife, all sins
cancelled, all facts sold
for life's sake. Being born
is strife, breaking into years
and battles, is time tried,
torn from hours of tears —
a dissonant music finding
its fool's harmony, pain
tender and filled with gold,
loss as gain, and a god's home.

ELEGY FOR AN UNKNOWN YOUTH

I stand inside of silence,
judging an ancient sorrow, measuring woe
as I would measure a river at flood
sweeping land and its habitations
down valleys in liquid darkness, slow.
Six runners, friends, shoulder you proudly
(on a winning day they'd
have borne you on cheers and laughter)
and place you unseen and shy
in your strict midnight suit alone
among candleflames bending and rising
as though your breath were there.
I stand inside of silence
with veiled women — darkly surrendered
wrack-strewn shores of a spent sea.
(Mother? Sisters? Lovers?)
Not wife, I'd guess. Your growth was tender
still for saying a binding yes.
Youth under the ivory pall, where
were you going when this way came to you?
Judging an ancient sorrow, measuring woe,
this requiem drama enacts us all.
We hear a secret intonation.
We will lie there, too.

MASS FOR KALI

Kyrie

On a raw night of riotous wind
I stumble alone pondering darkly.
"Waste . . . waste . . .", I whisper,
probing those years so
unresolved, fumbled, so running
down and no time now for repair.

Tumbling slow before my blinded eyes
came a tangle of patched gypsies,
turning, falling, weeping, turning,
coming to rest. "This is all?" I cry.
"Your tears to catch my heart
in unrelieved pity! Go!"

Rag-tag woman, animate grief,
lifts up a child with eyes of loss
and a fear-burned face. Easy
I take her to me across yearning
years. My arms are her place,
she, my child. And she smiles.

Gloria

Praise is of crashing, contrapuntal seas.
It is moonlight and a hare on snow.
Praise is love humming a heart like bees.

Praise is not soft. You must seize
it fiercely, dive to it, don't let go.
Praise is of crashing, contrapuntal seas.

It is orange butterflies swimming in breezes
of May. It is three robins in a row.
Praise is love humming a heart like bees.

Praise is struggle. It has no ease.
It shouts for sound, is stubborn, slow.
Praise is of crashing, contrapuntal seas.

It is a fire of falling autumn leaves,
a summer's worth of seeds to grow.
Praise is of crashing, contrapuntal seas,
praise is of love humming a heart like bees.

Credo

Innocence eternally dies at later equinox,
is raped, beaten, and dies,
is reaped, cut, pulled up, stacked, burned.
And then black candles and fierce marigolds
to speak Days of the Dead as eleven turns;
and all belongs to the young-old Queen of Death,
Mother of buried seeds. All flocks of innocence
are ingathered. Later, colder, each sunrise
caresses skeleton trees. We learn
through years of hope, anguish, that old
and new are only names for time's surprises
in this Mother's realm of ancient rocks
incised with naked bodies, hearts burned
on altars with erect, plumed, urgent stalks
of corn. Mother of Earth, starkly bold
in indifferent concern, You lead us to earn
our daily bread. Black dough lies
fecund under hands that ache and yearn

for respite. Don't leave us, Mother! Cold
and lost we are! "Work then," you say, "Turn
and knead and turn. It comes. It will rise
when you risk the fire." Mother of Rocks,
of Death, of Seed, if we can see Your eyes
bright with tears I think we can keep hold
of change, dying, suffering, rebirth, growing wise.

Sanctus

It was part of primeval rock,
a domed cube of mystery,
dark, frankincensed, empty,
dreaming its hesitant lights
frail as spring lilies.
He who came hieratic
in bright blood and gold robes,
was a fire older than Earth,
but serving, unnamed and obedient,
Her deaths and births. A vesture
he placed on me, foil-colored,
and filled my hands with wet soil.
"Evil will not stand", he said,
"if you work with your own clay.
Sanctify living this way alone."

Benedictus

blessing?   for what endurance?
not sign nor blessing shall ever be —
            only a sure rough bread
from servant   from whore

whose toughnesses find such freedoms
as others won't test   this Host
is black   coarse   ready
for breaking   for taking
into my very hands for they were led
into my hands, by the lowly taught
                to make,
and now   benedictus can be said

Agnus Dei

"I would have you endure a while.
You, what do you know?"
These ancient Nahuatl words
are arrows in me. Black,
bitter black, this place
where my fingers claw at rocks
and soil covering me,
pressing down upon my body.
What do I know?
Someone must be freed
to push green into sky,
to grow,
to sing firefly songs.
I see a young god flayed.
Pain occupies us.
He thrusts against earth as I do.
His is that coming birth
my wretchedness redeems!
It is to endure awhile
until life can frolic the grass,
not knowing surely who lives

but pushing blacknesses apart
for a god to pass.

GLORIA! Praise is of crashing earth and seas.
     Praise is love humming a heart like bees.

Ite, missa est.
DEPART, IT IS. I AM.

GOOD FRIDAY

Linnets sigh   cry bright sorrows
            in lonely time
try to tell colors of dappled love
colors of splashed April leaves
            of apple's snow
try to lift day and passion and pain
            to a god's bough.

This generous grass with buttercups
            is a couch
for dying on.   It is lonely
to die in flowers   more lonely than
            a desert sand death
because so lovely, lovely, harder to
            let go of rapture.

Crosses are turnings in lonely time
            fire-centered,
ancient rhymes chanting human, human,
            chanting changes
of plans   of seasons   of aging
of longed-for and slipped-away
            change of cyclonic pain.

Scratched blue behind slashed gold
            of a future
argues these hours of agony
of requiem   argues a new saying
            reborn   bold
as if living still had freedom
            or a life to weigh.

DONA EIS REQUIEM

Give them rest?
Why?
With so many tree tips
to make gay hurdles for leaping
into a sky of porcelain nextness
and cerulean space?
Rest?
Rather shall they climb
this air, slide down green hills,
mount clouds, be kingfishers,
dive into the sea,
come wet and laughing to run
in the sandy sun
to death's lonely lover's
wild undoing hands!

SEVEN LAST WORDS

"Forgive"

That pit of unintent
where all things are forfeited
gapes at earth's feet.
I stumble in, surprised,
incompetent, unfit to hold
this cavalier quail
    while his pertness sags
    to death,
my hands and his glazed eyes
    composing a ruin.

Is there forgiveness in him
who might yet be pacing his covey,
rolling and rustling uphill,
    had not my window in and
    my imagination out
    been inequivalent?
How could he tell, exploding
with nurture that he would die
    against a glass sky?
    I didn't intend it.
His covey slides away.

We are left, we two, in this pit
where all is forfeit —
    he incorrupt, and I
weighted with malefaction and
a mastery as profitless as Cain's.
Can my sight be opened, my naivete be
recommended to mercy,

my grief be made proper?
What amnesty is possible
for being human?

"Forsaken"

Terrible, terrible is black spring,
a terrible apocalyptic rider of death
across April, as if wild iris,
buttercups, lilacs and locust trees
opulent with bees and blossoms were
    vanity. As if all were vanity.
A cloud of aloneness stands
    between us and our God,
a cloud thick-doomed, grief at its core.
    We cannot find each other —
we because we feel forsaken entire,
that One because, lacking our voice,
    no creation can shout for joy.
To be nailed under such mandate of
    silence and passion
    (for how can be told that pain,
    unwatered, of our particular
    decrease of bright love which
    could gleam a world?)
to hang so dulled and nowhere is
to have played child and been repaid
    sums of obscurity.
This harsh knurled tree at our back
    is truer than justice.
Linnets gone, can we reconcile this night?

"Thirst"

Plovers cry over ploughed fields
before dawn as if they too had dreams,
as if they too awoke in darkness,
    fearing an incubus upon them,
fleeing as wraiths of the unsanctified.
    They speak my voice.
They speed my terror on their sharp
swift wings, while I
    against silenced eyes watch
    plunging of souls to wasteland,
two by two, twined woman to man in
clutching unbelief that despair is
    one of the savories of God.
I cannot constrain them in their fall.
    They are my own.
Whatever place of bones and ground
they reach, whatever path of withering
they walk, my feet make their footsteps
    and their tongues cleave
    to the roof of my mouth.
Our thirst, huge as genesis, will not
be eased till human darkness be compassed,
gentled with adoption,
    held holy and remembered
    as first countenance of light.

"Woman Behold"

I, being woman, am much beset
by substance, by alchemy of blood
and bone, by wild fields
whose indiscriminate largesse requires
more from me,
    more of birth, more of dying,
than I had thought
I could stretch out for.
Seeing a face crumple under pain,
or rearrange itself behind walls
    when a dream drowns,
I ask if it is harder for women
to encompass anguish of endless
    dissolution and endless return?
    Or easier?
Or is it that our knowing is
neither harder nor easier but other,
    built upon tides, not rocks?
Each has its nails and its specific
    agony. I, being woman,
must take mine to a midnight womb,
teach it solitude and help it
    give itself away.
Mothers of mystery, sons of dream,
let mother to son and son to mother
    be an eternal turning,
    reciprocal beholding
which keeps us and cosmos, substance
and spirit, face to urgent face.

"In Paradise"

This is our garden:
   one rose past plenitude
   hangs listless and estranged,
its petals curled to a disk of dry stamens.
Somewhere beyond a dove speaks minorly.
   For the rest, it is green and
   singing and does not matter.
The air is stifling with recall, upstart
are leaves, and finch's love song
   strikes like wrath.
We are between sin and what is
unconceived, siblings to those two
who fled naked on a day of disobedience.
   We the exiles, robbers, thieves,
   our innocence dispersed as mist,
   hang in sun's command,
   no way back from time.
Pierced by dying, our hands mourn
   as we consider our dead —
lost voices, almost remembered faces,
heads turned listening, other-seeing
eyes, feet placed just so on uneven ground.
   Dove moves forever in garden shadow,
   breath-quiet. Petals fall.

"Into Those Hands"

It seems simple to lift our lives up
to light, seeing how threadbare and
ragged they are, and to say hopefully
    to tolerant angels,
    "Make this yours."
Childhood's canyons of laurel-scented
sunlight are distant, pulses of
twenty quieted, and middle years might
prosper under angelic dominance.
    It is harder but more accurate
to see life fastened by a leash of longing
to naked Omnipotence Who takes us
    down corridors of chaos,
    does not steady us when we stumble,
    tugs ropes and waits
for our cut feet to falter forward through
a night rubbled and smelling of pain.
    We cannot give life away
as do children or the very old.
    We must bear it with us,
commit it to whatever shapes matter
to purposes of Its own, as thunder
shapes air and as lightning leaps chasms
    to remake each universe.